This book belongs to _____ Age _____

Favourite player _____

Prediction of Coventry's final position this season _____

Prediction of Sky Bet League 1 winners this season _____

Prediction of FA Cup winners this season _____

Prediction of Capital One Cup winners this season _____

Prediction of teams to be promoted
to the Sky Bet Championship this season:

1st _____

2nd _____

Play Off Winners _____

Written by twocan

Contributors: Mark Hornby, Carl Newell & Rob Mason

A TWOCAN PUBLICATION

©2013. Published by twocan
under licence from Coventry City FC.

Every effort has been made to ensure the accuracy
of information within this publication but the publishers can not
be held responsible for any errors or omissions. Views expressed
are those of the author and do not necessarily represent those
of the publishers or the football club. All rights reserved.

ISBN 978-1-909872-02-8

PICTURE CREDITS
Press Association & Action Images

£7.50

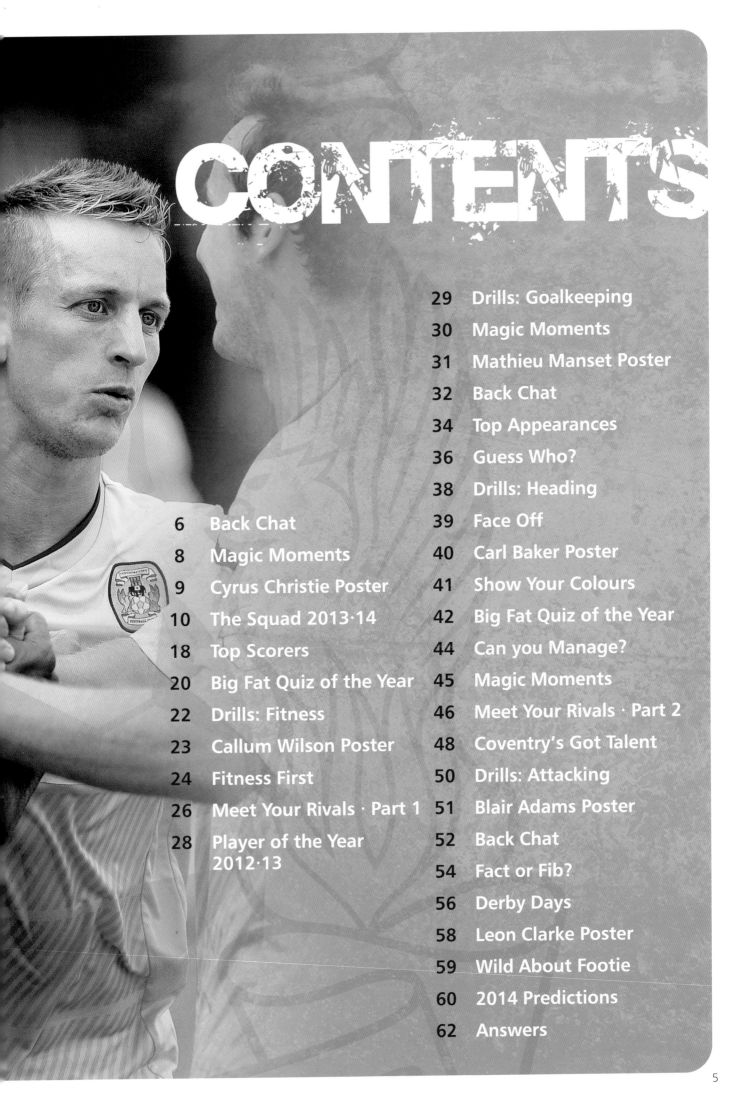

CONTENTS

CARL BAKER

FAVOURITES

Favourite actor?
Samuel L Jackson

Favourite actress? Angelina Jolie

Favourite movie? Shawshank Redemption

Favourite musician or band? The Beatles

Favourite place? Dubai

YOUR TEAM MATES

Who is the best trainer? **Conor Thomas**

Who has the worst dress sense? **Billy Daniels**

Who is the best dancer?

Jordan Willis

Who is the joker in the dressing room?

Leon Clarke

Who spends longest in front of the mirror?

Jordan Clarke

If you could trade places with someone for a day, who would it be?
Adam Sandler

What do you do on your days off?
Golfing

Snow or Sun?
Coffee or tea?
Early bird or night owl?
Action or comedy?
Apple or Blackberry?
Cowboys or aliens?
Skiing or Snowboarding?
Sausage or bacon?
Cats or dogs?
Bond or Bourne?

What are your pet hates?
Loads! Untidiness is the number one

If not a footballer, what would you be?
Golfer

If you were a character in any movie, who would it be?
Superman

BACK CHAT

LEON CLARKE

FAVOURITES

Favourite actor? Denzel Washington

Favourite actress? Eva Mendes

Favourite movie? White Men Can't Jump

Favourite musician or band? Tyga

Favourite place? America

YOUR TEAM MATES

Who is the best trainer? Carl Baker

Who has the worst dress sense? Joe Murphy

Who is the best dancer? Mathieu Manset

Who is the joker in the dressing room? Callum Wilson

Who spends longest in front of the mirror? Jordan Clarke

If you were a character in any movie, who would it be? Jake from Avatar

What are your pet hates? Bad odour

If you could trade places with someone for a day, who would it be? Lebron James

Snow or (Sun?)

Coffee or (tea?)

Early bird or (night owl?)

Action or (comedy?)

(Apple) or Blackberry?

Cowboys or (aliens?)

Skiing or (Snowboarding?)

(Sausage) or bacon?

Cats or (dogs?)

(Bond) or Bourne?

JORDAN CLARKE

FAVOURITES

Favourite actor? Denzel Washington

Favourite actress? Eva Mendes

Favourite movie? Think Like A Man

Favourite musician or band? Drake Or J Cole

Favourite place? Home

YOUR TEAM MATES

Who is the best trainer? Cyrus Christie

Who has the worst dress sense? Callum Wilson

Who is the best dancer? Mathieu Manset

Who is the joker in the dressing room? Callum Wilson

Who spends longest in front of the mirror? Carl Baker

What are your pet hates? People being late

If you could trade places with someone for a day, who would it be? Ashton Kutcher

What do you do on your days off? Play COD on PS3 with Conor, Cyrus and Callum

Snow or (Sun?)

Coffee or (tea?)

Early bird or (night owl?)

Action or comedy? bit of both

(Apple) or Blackberry?

Cowboys or (aliens?)

(Skiing) or Snowboarding?

(Sausage) or bacon? all day!

Cats or (dogs?) but I have a cat!

(Bond) or Bourne?

MAGIC MOMENTS

1987 FA Cup Win

16TH MAY 1987

Against the odds, Coventry City won the 1987 FA Cup on a sunny May day at Wembley. Managed by John Sillett & George Curtis, the Sky Blues beat the favourites Tottenham Hotspur 3-2 after extra time in a classic final watched by 98,000 in the stadium.

The Sky Blues had to come from behind, as Clive Allen scored his 49th goal of the season to put Spurs ahead after 2 minutes. However, they pegged back the opposition almost immediately as winger Dave Bennett rounded the keeper and found the net after a Keith Houchen knock down.

Spurs took a 2-1 lead just before half time, when Chris Waddle's free kick caused confusion in the Coventry defence and the ball hit Tottenham's Gary Mabbutt and deflected in the Sky Blues goal.

The end-to-end nature of the match continued in the second half and Coventry City scored one of the most memorable goals in FA Cup history 17 minutes into it as Houchen's full-length diving header connected with Bennett's cross and both scores were level.

Thirty minutes of extra time was required to separate the sides and the deadlock was broken for the final time in the 95th minute as Lloyd McGrath's cross hit the knee of Gary Mabbutt and the ball looped over the despairing hand of Spurs keeper Ray Clemence, leaving the Sky Blues 3-2 ahead.

The Sky Blues defence battled bravely to see out the final 25 minutes of the match, with Steve Ogrizovic keeping the Spurs strikeforce at bay. Eventually, the final whistle blew and the Sky Blues claimed the first piece of major silverware in our history. Captain Brian Kilcline lifted the trophy to prompt the fans who came down from Coventry into jubilation and BBC Commentator John Motson to say 'The Sky Blues are sky high!'

2 CYRUS CHRISTIE

1

Joe Murphy

Position: Goalkeeper
Nationality: Irish
DOB: 21.08.81
Height: 6' 2"
Weight: 12st 8lb

The Republic of Ireland international joined the ranks of the Sky Blues on a three-year deal in July 2011. He has been No.1 choice for the goalkeeper position ever since!

2

Cyrus Christie

Position: Defender
Nationality: English
DOB: 30.09.92
Height: 6' 2"
Weight: 12st 4lb

Academy product Cyrus is one of the Sky Blues' most consistent performers and won Young Player of the Year last season.

Blair Adams

Position: Defender
Nationality: English
DOB: 08.09.91
Height: 5' 11"
Weight: 11st 5lb

Adams is a talented left back who holds two caps at England Under-20 level!

3

THE SQUAD 2013·14

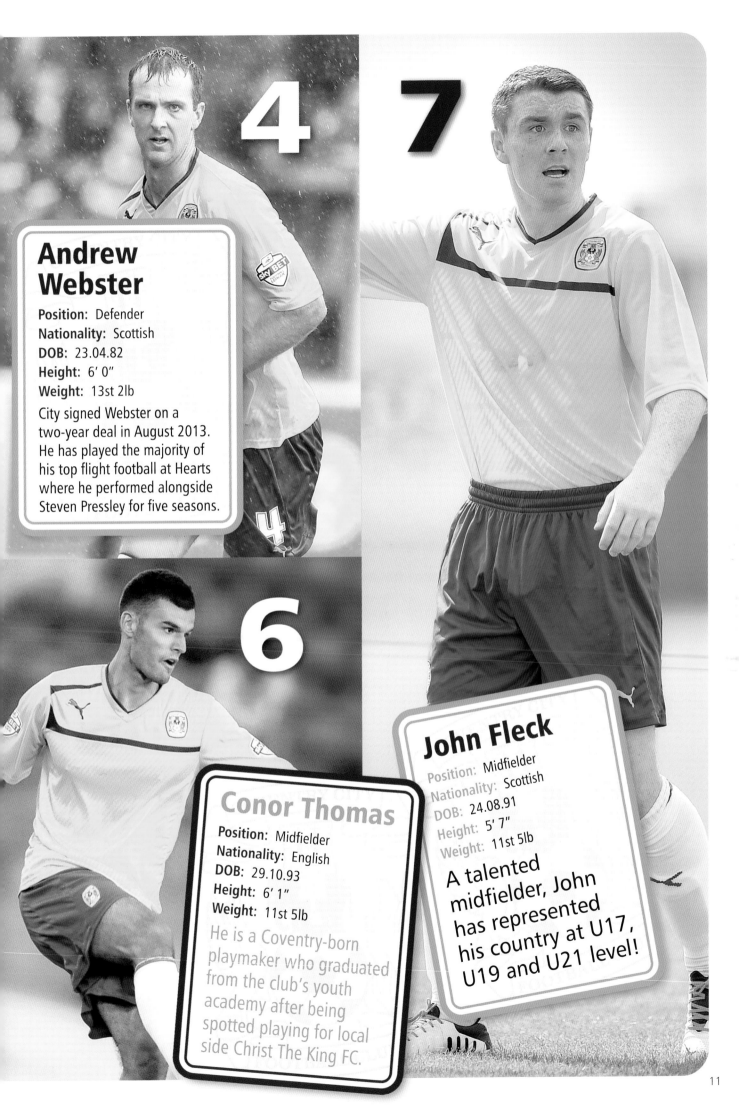

4

Andrew Webster

Position: Defender
Nationality: Scottish
DOB: 23.04.82
Height: 6' 0"
Weight: 13st 2lb

City signed Webster on a two-year deal in August 2013. He has played the majority of his top flight football at Hearts where he performed alongside Steven Pressley for five seasons.

7

John Fleck

Position: Midfielder
Nationality: Scottish
DOB: 24.08.91
Height: 5' 7"
Weight: 11st 5lb

A talented midfielder, John has represented his country at U17, U19 and U21 level!

6

Conor Thomas

Position: Midfielder
Nationality: English
DOB: 29.10.93
Height: 6' 1"
Weight: 11st 5lb

He is a Coventry-born playmaker who graduated from the club's youth academy after being spotted playing for local side Christ The King FC.

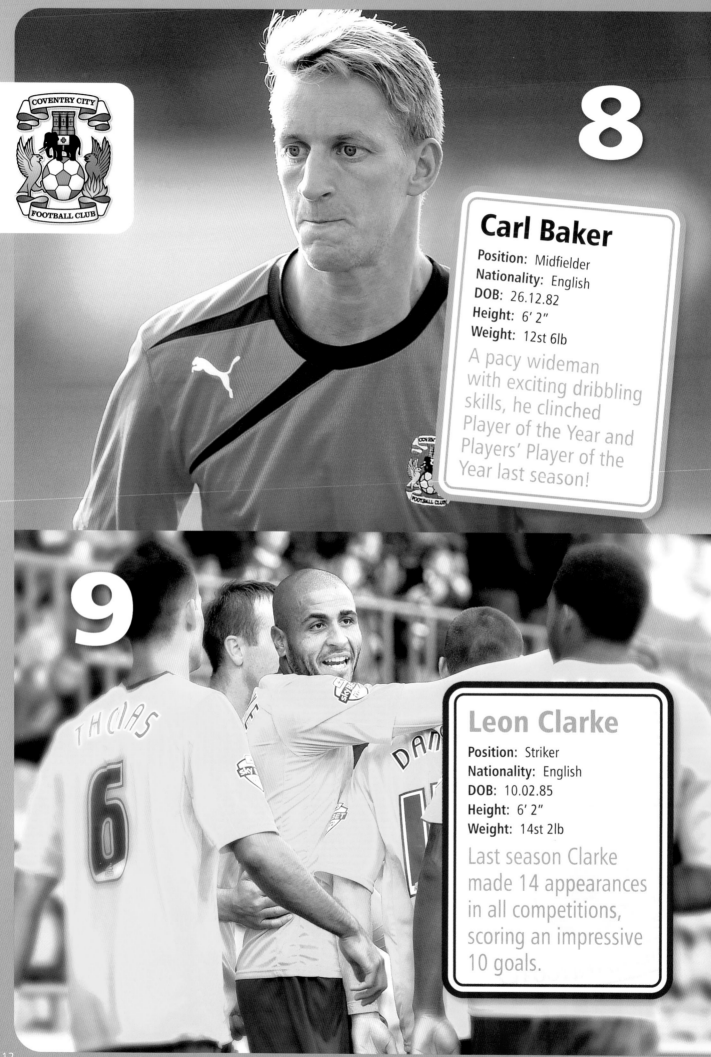

8

Carl Baker

Position: Midfielder
Nationality: English
DOB: 26.12.82
Height: 6' 2"
Weight: 12st 6lb

A pacy wideman with exciting dribbling skills, he clinched Player of the Year and Players' Player of the Year last season!

9

Leon Clarke

Position: Striker
Nationality: English
DOB: 10.02.85
Height: 6' 2"
Weight: 14st 2lb

Last season Clarke made 14 appearances in all competitions, scoring an impressive 10 goals.

10

13

Lee Burge

Position: Goalkeeper
Nationality: English
DOB: 09.01.93
Height: 5'11"
Weight: 11st

Lee Burge came through the Sky Blues' youth academy. He is yet to make a first team appearance but was a mainstay in goal while on loan at Nuneaton Town last season.

Mathieu Manset

Position: Striker
Nationality: French
DOB: 05.08.89
Height: 6' 1"
Weight: 13st 8lb

Coventry signed Manset on a one-year deal in August 2013 and was Steven Pressley's first signing in summer 2013!

14

Franck Moussa

Position: Midfielder
Nationality: Belgian
DOB: 24.07.89
Height: 5' 8"
Weight: 12st 8lb

Moussa signed for the Sky Blues in September 2012 and quickly established himself as a fans' favourite, having made 46 appearances last season, scoring six goals.

16

17

Adam Barton

Position: Midfielder
Nationality: English
DOB: 07.01.91
Height: 5' 11"
Weight: 12st 2lb

The talented, young midfielder has already been capped by Northern Ireland!

Billy Daniels

Position: Midfielder
Nationality: English
DOB: 03.07.94
Height: 6' 0"
Weight: 11st 7lb

A midfielder or striker, Daniels came through the Academy ranks before becoming part of the first team squad in 2013.

18

Aaron Phillips

Position: Defender
Nationality: English
DOB: 20.11.93
Height: 5'8"
Weight: 11st 2lbs

Aaron is the son of Sky Blues 1987 FA Cup winner Dave Phillips and spent the end of the 2012-13 season on loan at Nuneaton Town.

19

Jordan Willis

Position: Defender
Nationality: English
DOB: 24.08.94
Height: 5' 11"
Weight: 11st

Willis signed a pro deal in May 2012 after impressing in the Academy side and received England U19 & 18 call ups.

20

Callum Wilson

Position: Striker
Nationality: English
DOB: 27.02.92
Height: 5' 11"
Weight: 10st 6lb

Wilson is a pacy product of the Sky Blues' academy and scored his first goal for the club on 12 March 2013, in a 2-2 draw at home to Colchester United.

24

Jordan Clarke

Position: Defender
Nationality: English
DOB: 19.11.91
Height: 6′ 0″
Weight: 11st 3lb

Clarke has represented England at U19 and U20 level! He played a large part in helping England advance to the elite qualification round for the 2010 European Championships.

30

Louis Garner

Position: Midfielder
Nationality: English
DOB: 31.10.94
Height: 5′ 10″
Weight: 11st 7lb

Garner signed a one-year deal with the club in July 2013 after impressing for the Under-21s last season.

Ryan Haynes

Position: Defender
Nationality: English
DOB: 27.09.95
Height: 5′ 7″
Weight: 10st 10lb

Academy graduate Ryan made his first start for the club against Brentford in April 2013.

31

33

Leon Lobjoit

Position: Midfielder
Nationality: English
DOB: 04.01.95
Height: 6' 2"
Weight: 12st 10lb

The club offered Leon his first pro deal in July 2013 after he impressed in the Academy system and the Under-21s last season.

32

Ben Maund

Position: Striker
Nationality: English
DOB: 07.05.95
Height: 5' 7"
Weight: 11st 11lb

The 18-year old made several impressive performances for the Under-21s last season, which led to his first professional deal in football.

34

Alex Gott

Position: Goalkeeper
Nationality: English
DOB: 30.09.95
Height: 6' 1"
Weight: 11st 6lb

Academy Graduate, Gott was given a squad number at the start of the 2013/14 season and will look to develop his game while 3rd choice keeper for the Sky Blues in the coming season.

Lewis Rankin

Position: Midfielder
Nationality: English
DOB: 02.07.1995
Height: 5' 7"
Weight: 9st 6lbs

Rankin is a product of the club's Academy system and will be looking to progress through the Development squad this season.

35

1 Clarrie Bourton

1931-1937 · 182 GOALS

Bourton was a centre-forward, who could also play out on the wing. Bristol-born, after a spell with his hometown club he moved to Blackburn where his prolific form in Lancashire led to his transfer to Coventry.

TOP

Manager Harry Storer signed him for £750, and he scored 49 goals in his first season with the club - a figure which is still a record in a season for a Coventry City player. In Bourton's six seasons at Highfield Road, Coventry scored 577 league goals and he weighed in with 171 of them.

A bustling, old-style striker, his play was very much suited to the Third Division but found goals tougher to come by in the higher divisions. He left in 1937 for Plymouth Argyle, before a move back to his hometown club of Bristol City. Bourton retired from football in 1944, and was employed by the club in the pools office until shortly before his death in 1981.

2

SCORERS

Billy Lake
1928-1939 · 123 Goals

Lake was one of the unsung heroes of the 1930s. He was the longest-serving player of the inter-war era, spending 11 seasons with the club. Though over-shadowed by Bourton, he was prolific in his own right - scoring on average a goal every other game and retired upon the outbreak of war in 1939.

JOINT 3RD

Frank Herbert
1922-1929 · 86 Goals

Frank Herbert was one of Highfield Road's most popular and prolific players in the 1920s. A miner, he began his career in local football before signing for Coventry in 1922. He played either left-wing or inside-left, but wherever he played the goals kept coming.

JOINT 3RD

Ted Roberts
1936-1952 · 86 Goals

A player with superb heading ability, Roberts was unfortunate in that his career was interrupted by the Second World War. However, in his 212 league games he was a vital part of the side and often seen as a big 'team player' whose goals and general play helped the club greatly.

Ray Straw
1957-1961 · 85 Goals

Billy Firth brought in Straw to try to rescue the club from relegation to Division Four. While he didn't manage to save the team, his goals in the next season helped an immediate return to Division Three and he maintained form in following seasons. Not blessed with great pace, he could shoot with both feet and was a terrific header of the ball.

5

BIG FAT QUIZ
OF THE YEAR

01 JANUARY

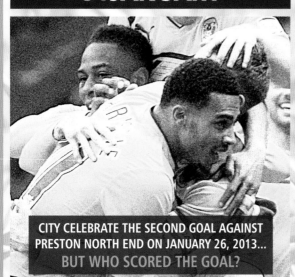

CITY CELEBRATE THE SECOND GOAL AGAINST PRESTON NORTH END ON JANUARY 26, 2013...
BUT WHO SCORED THE GOAL?

Leon Clarke had his 28th birthday on 10th February 2013...

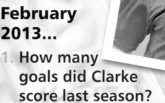

1. How many goals did Clarke score last season?

2. Leon is a towering 6'6". True or False?

3. Where did Clarke start his professional career?

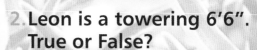

02 FEBRUARY

03 MARCH

Steven Pressley was announced as the new manager of League One side Coventry City on 8 March 2013.

1. What team did he manage before Coventry?

2. Steven Pressley was born in Wales. True or False?

3. Pressley spent most of his playing career at Hearts.

How many appearances did he make?

WHO SCORED HIS SIDE'S SECOND GOAL OF THE GAME AGAINST NOTTS COUNTY IN APRIL 2013?

04APRIL

05MAY

1. Coventry City won the FA Cup against Tottenham Hotspur in May 1987, but what was the score?

2. Who was the Manager of City when they won the FA Cup?

3. Which three players scored the goals?

4. The match was played at Wembley. What was the attendance?

5. Who was Coventry's goalie at the time?

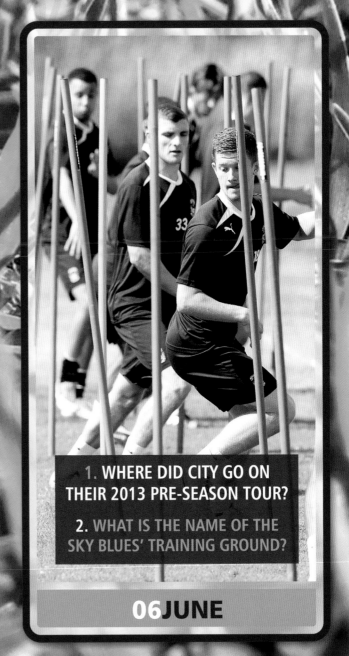

1. WHERE DID CITY GO ON THEIR 2013 PRE-SEASON TOUR?

2. WHAT IS THE NAME OF THE SKY BLUES' TRAINING GROUND?

06JUNE

ANSWERS ON PAGE 62

You will need cones or markers, a ball and a friend!

Shuttle runs are a great fitness training exercise to help build speed, stamina, acceleration and endurance. Adding a football helps players control the ball at top speeds and when the body is tired.

EASY

Set up a line of 6-8 cones 5 metres apart. To begin with, run from the first cone to the second cone and back again. Next, run to the second cone and back again. Continue to do this until you have completed a run to the final cone.

HARD

Now, add a football into the mix!

Dribble from the start to the first cone, turn with the ball, pass back to your friend and then sprint back to the start. Your friend should stop the ball at the start where you will gain possession and dribble to the second cone. Repeat this process for each of the cones.

Have your friend throw the ball to you as you're running back to the start. You will have to work to bring the ball under control, bring it back to the start and dribble on to the next cone - work on chest traps, thigh traps or traps with the feet.

As you improve, try and work faster. Can you invent some of your own ways to make this drill harder?

HARDER

There are many ways you can increase the difficulty level of this drill.

Remember to swap roles with your friend so you both get a chance to work on your fitness!

START

DRILLS: FITNESS

20CALLUM WILSON

23

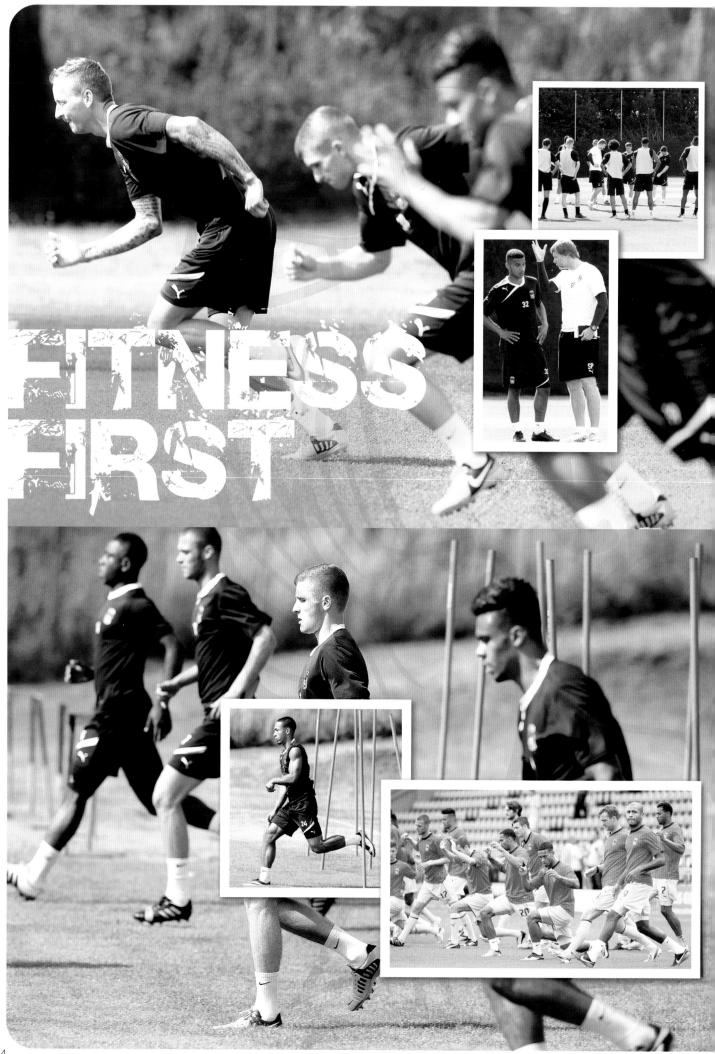

FITNESS FIRST

Footballers are top athletes. In order to stay at the top of their game they need to be supremely fit. Unlike fantastic sports such as athletics, cricket, tennis or basketball for instance, football is a contact sport. This means that as well as injuries that can be picked up through strains or pulls, footballers have to deal with the rough and tumble of applying their skills when they often only have a split second between gaining possession of the ball and having to withstand a challenge.

Once footballers hear the final whistle, attention swiftly turns to the next game which in League One usually comes every few days. The result of this is that not only do players have to be fantastically fit but they have to perform time and time again with at least 46 games to be played each season; more if teams do not lose at the first hurdle in the cup competitions.

Footballers do a lot of running, weight training and swimming. They might also go cycling and more and more clubs now get players to 'box-er-cise' which involves a lot of routines normally done by boxers. Pilates and Yoga can also be beneficial for players because such activities help to stretch muscles, assist with back problems and increase body strength.

Most of the hard work by players is carried out in the pre-season period. This is when fitness and conditioning coaches work on building up players so that they can perform for 90 minutes against a team of opponents all of whom they can expect to be super-fit too.

Once the season gets going, most clubs train for around two hours a day with much of the training based on actually playing, particularly focussing on the next match they have to play. It is important that during the season, players don't over-train. Rest and recuperation can be as important as a weights session because fitness coaches have to ensure player performance peaks for match day.

MEET YOUR RIVALS PART 1

BRADFORD CITY

Ground: Valley Parade **Capacity:** 25,136
Manager: Phil Parkinson **Nicknames:** The Bantams, The Paraders, The Citizens **Did you know:** In 2013 they became the first ever 4th tier team to reach a major domestic Wembley Cup Final - the Football League Cup.

BRENTFORD

Ground: Griffin Park **Capacity:** 12,300
Manager: Uwe Rösler **Nickname:** The Bees
Did you know: Brentford's most successful spell came during the 1930s, when they achieved consecutive top six finishes in the First Division.

BRISTOL CITY

Ground: Ashton Gate **Capacity:** 21,501
Manager: Sean O'Driscoll
Nicknames: The Robins, The Reds, Cider Army
Did you know: F1 driver Jenson Button and actor Russell Crowe are both fans of Bristol City.

CARLISLE UNITED

Ground: Brunton Park **Capacity:** 18,202
Manager: Greg Abbott **Nicknames:** Cumbrians, Blues
Did you know: Carlisle is the smallest location, by population, to have had a resident top flight English football club since 1906.

COLCHESTER UNITED

Ground: Colchester Community Stadium
Capacity: 10,084 **Manager:** Joe Dunne
Nickname: The U's **Did you know:** Colchester United are perhaps most famous for beating Leeds United 3-2 in the 5th round of the FA Cup in 1971.

CRAWLEY TOWN

Ground: Broadfield Stadium **Capacity:** 5,996
Manager: Richie Barker **Nicknames:** The Reds,
Red Devils **Did you know:** Crawley Town's
historical rivals are Aldershot Town and Woking,
however they also dislike Brighton & Hove Albion.

CREWE ALEXANDRA

Ground: Alexandra Stadium **Capacity:** 10,153
Manager: Steve Davis
Nicknames: The Railwaymen, The Alex
Did you know: Crewe's only major honour is the
Football League Trophy which they won in 2013.

GILLINGHAM

Ground: Priestfield Stadium **Capacity:** 11,582
Manager: Martin Allen **Nickname:** The Gills
Did you know: Between 2000 and 2005,
Gillingham were in the 2nd tier for the
only time in their history!

LEYTON ORIENT

Ground: Matchroom Stadium **Capacity:** 9,271
Manager: Russell Slade **Nicknames:** The O's,
Orient **Did you know:** Orient finished 7th,
one place away from the play-off positions,
in both the 2010-11 and 2012-13 seasons.

MK DONS

Ground: Stadium mk **Capacity:** 22,000
Manager: Karl Robinson **Nickname:** The Dons
Did you know: MK Dons were founded very
recently, on 21 June 2004, nine months after
Wimbledon FC's relocation to Milton Keynes.

NOTTS COUNTY

Ground: Meadow Lane **Capacity:** 20,229
Manager: Chris Kiwomya **Nickname:** The
Magpies **Did you know:** Formed on 28 November
1862, Notts County are the oldest football team in
the world to currently play at a professional level.

Coventry City captain and midfielder Carl Baker scooped the Player of the Year award for the 2012/13 season, adding to the Top Goalscorer and Players' Player of the Year awards, which he won for his impressive exploits last season.

Baker was a constant presence in the Sky Blues side, making 56 appearances in all competitions and scoring 15 goals. Not only did he find the back of the net but he also made key contributions to his team's attacking play, claiming 13 assists in all competitions, and his work rate contributed hugely to the team's overall performances.

Over the season Baker also built up an impressive partnership with right back Cyrus Christie, which arguably brought out the best in the two right sided players. On many occasions, the pair would double up both in attack and defence to create problems for the opposition.

The 29-year old's committed, all action approach has won the hearts and appreciation of many Sky Blues fans, helping him to get 58% of the Player of the Year vote.

Baker joined Coventry City in the 2010 January transfer window from Stockport County. His career up until that point had included spells at Southport and Morecambe, where he had developed a reputation as an attacking midfielder with an eye for a spectacular goal. Signed by then manager Chris Coleman, he was praised for his mazy runs and direct style, which brought variation to the way the Sky Blues played at that time.

In his first two full seasons at the Sky Blues, Baker struggled to get on the scoresheet regularly. However during the 2012/13 season he was awarded the captaincy of the side, and this move seemed to spur the Liverpudlian onto greater all round performances, ultimately leading to Baker becoming even more of a fans' favourite and Player of the Year for the 2012/13 season.

2012·13 PLAYER OF THE YEAR

Set up three cones in a large triangle. These become our three goals! Make sure the triangle is big enough for the goalie to dive around in.

The goalie stands in the centre of the triangle and three shooters stand opposite the three goals at their 'penalty spots'.

EASY

To start with, the shooters take it in turns to fire shots past the goalie - the goalie must work quickly to reposition himself for the next shot.

HARD

Players then start to fire shots more quickly. Just as the goalkeeper recovers from the last shot, the next player quickly shoots again.

HARDER

Change the order in which the shooters take their shots. Shooters shout their names in any order, to signal that they are going to shoot. This keeps the goalie on his toes.

Also, be sure to try different shots - high, low, left foot, right foot, maybe even try chipping the ball over the keeper's head!

DRILLS: GOALKEEPING

MAGIC MOMENTS

Coventry City 6-2 Derby County

FINAL GAME AT HIGHFIELD ROAD · 30TH APRIL 2005

Coventry City said goodbye to their Highfield Road home of 106 years in some style as they thrashed Derby County 6-2 and secured their Championship survival in the process.

The performance was unexpected against a Derby side pushing for the play-offs and was clearly their best performance of the season, rounding off a memorable day tinged with sadness. Legends of Highfield Road were in attendance including former manager Jimmy Hill, who led the sell-out crowd in singing the Sky Blue Song before the match. Within 40 minutes of the match kicking off, the Sky Blues were 4-0 up and a party atmosphere was in full flow thanks to two goals from local lad Gary McShefferey, plus strikes from Dele Adebola and Stern John.

Derby fought back in the second half but it was not enough as John made it five, before Andrew Whing sealed his place in Coventry City history when the ball dropped to the full back on the edge of the Derby box. Whing, not known for his goalscoring antics, caught the ball well and it flew into the roof of the net, sparking frantic celebrations.

Following the final whistle and the referee drawing to a close 106 years of memories, there was one final rendition of the Sky Blue song as fans entered onto the pitch and savoured their final moments at their home.

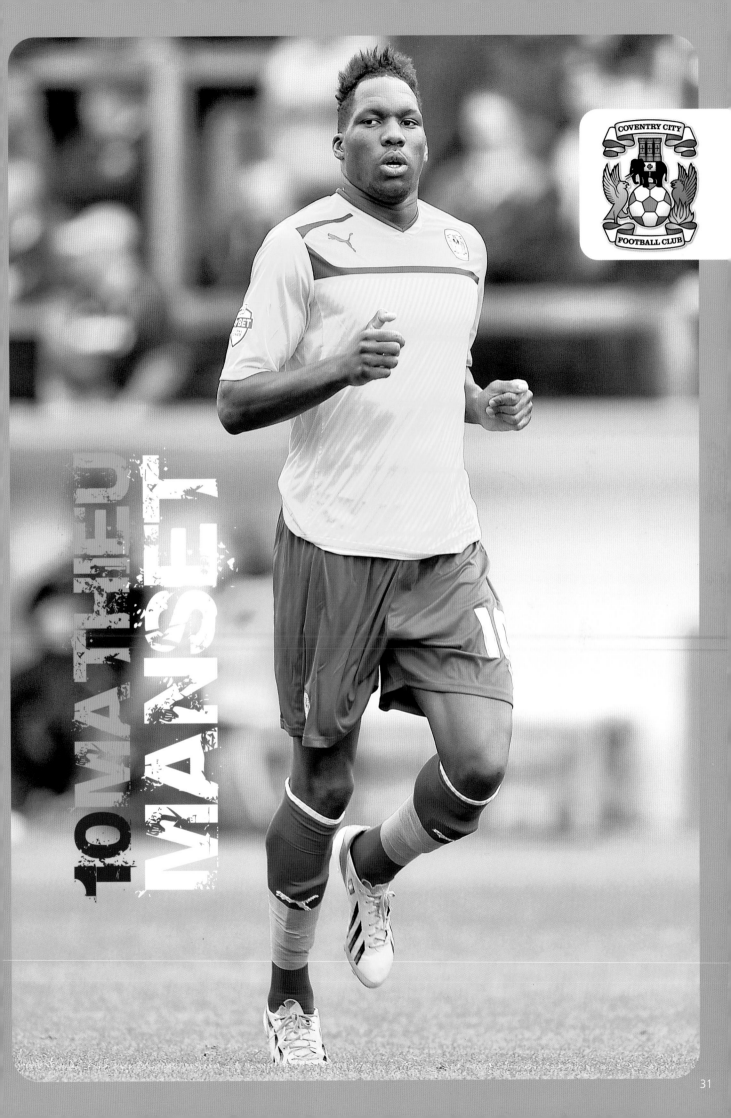

10 MATHIEU MANSET

FRANCK MOUSSA

FAVOURITES

Favourite actor? **Kirk Cameron**

Favourite actress? Keri Washington

Favourite movie? **Remember The Titans**

Favourite musician or band? Trip Lee

Favourite place? **London**

YOUR TEAM MATES

Who is the best trainer? **Cyrus Christie**

Who has the worst dress sense? **Lee Burge**

Who is the best dancer? **Mathieu Manset**

Who is the joker in the dressing room? **Callum Wilson**

Who spends longest in front of the mirror? **Jordan Clarke**

If you were a character in any movie, who would it be? Marty McFly

If you could trade places with someone for a day, who would it be? Pele at WCF 1962

BACK CHAT

Snow or Sun?
Coffee or tea?
Early bird or night owl?
Action or comedy?
Apple or Blackberry?
Cowboys or aliens?
Skiing or Snowboarding?
Sausage or bacon?
Cats or dogs?
Bond or Bourne?

What are your pet hates? **Traffic**

What are your pet hates? People talking through a film

If you could trade places with someone for a day, who would it be? Tiger Woods

If not a footballer, what would you be? Bricklayer or Carpenter

Snow or Sun?
Coffee or tea?
Early bird or night owl?
Action or comedy?
Apple or Blackberry?
Cowboys or aliens?
Skiing or Snowboarding?
Sausage or bacon?
Cats or dogs?
Bond or Bourne?

JOE MURPHY

FAVOURITES

Favourite actor? **Denzel Washington**

Favourite actress? **Hilary Swank**

Favourite movie? **Shawshank Redemption**

Favourite musician or band? **U2**

Favourite place? **Home**

YOUR TEAM MATES

Who is the best trainer? **Franck Moussa**

Who has the worst dress sense? **Conor Thomas. Loves a tracksuit.**

Who is the best dancer? **Me**

Who is the joker in the dressing room? **Blair Adams. Great Banter.**

Who spends longest in front of the mirror? **Jordan Clarke**

ANDREW WEBSTER

FAVOURITES

Favourite actor? **Nicolas Cage**

Favourite actress? **Angelina Jolie**

Favourite movie? **Olympus Has Fallen**

Favourite musician or band? **Oasis**

Favourite place? **Home**

YOUR TEAM MATES

Who is the best trainer? Me

Who has the worst dress sense? Leon Lobjoit

Who is the best dancer? Definitely not me! Not seen the others dance yet

Who is the joker in the dressing room? Murphy

Who spends longest in front of the mirror? Not seen anyone man marking the mirror to be fair

If you were a character in any movie, who would it be? William Wallace

Snow or **Sun?**
Coffee or tea?
Early bird or night owl?
Action or comedy?
Apple or Blackberry?
Cowboys or aliens?
Skiing or Snowboarding?
Sausage or bacon?
Cats or **dogs?**
Bond or Bourne?

If not a footballer, what would you be? Something intellectual

What do you do on your days off? Spend time with family

What are your pet hates? When someone leaves the last bit of milk

If not a footballer, what would you be? Sports Coach

If you were a character in any movie, who would it be? Justin Timberlake in Friends with Benefits

Snow or **Sun?**
Coffee or tea?
Early bird or **night owl?**
Action or **comedy?**
Apple or Blackberry?
Cowboys or **aliens?**
Skiing or Snowboarding?
Sausage or bacon?
Cats or **dogs?**
Bond or Bourne?

CONOR THOMAS

FAVOURITES

Favourite actor? **Mark Wahlberg**

Favourite actress? **Mila Kunis**

Favourite movie? **Think Like A Man**

Favourite musician or band? **Drake**

Favourite place? **LA**

YOUR TEAM MATES

Who is the best trainer? **Carl Baker**

Who has the worst dress sense? **Jordan Clarke**

Who is the best dancer? **Jordan Willis**

Who is the joker in the dressing room? **Callum Wilson**

Who spends longest in front of the mirror? **Jordan Clarke**

33

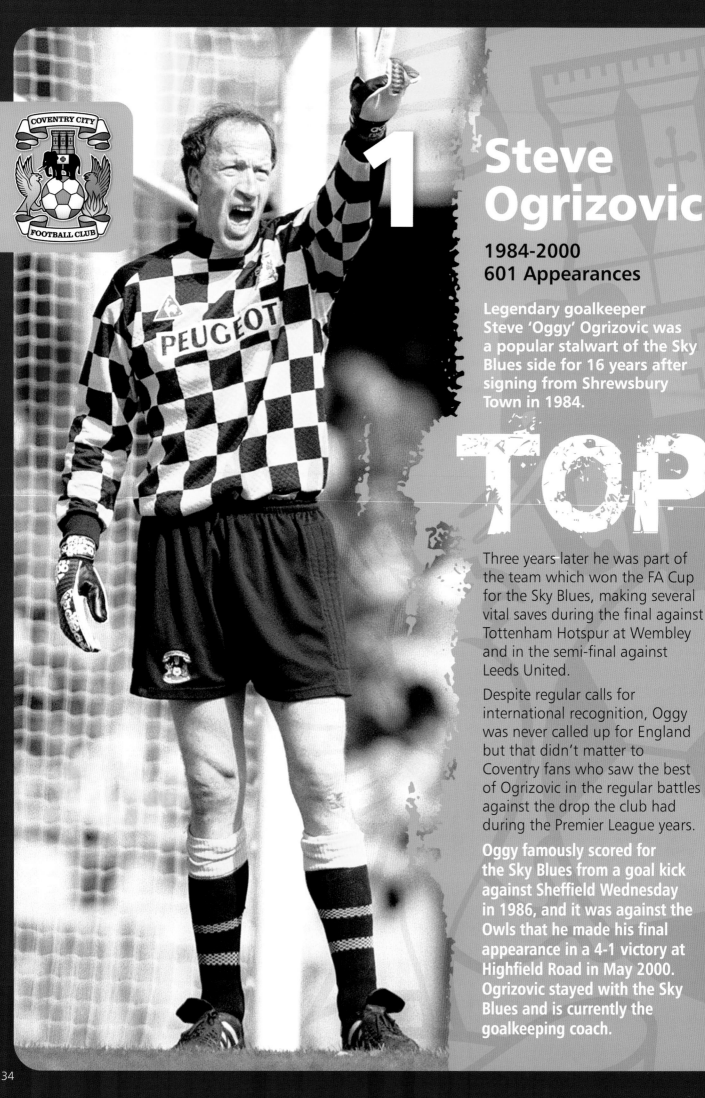

1

Steve Ogrizovic

1984-2000
601 Appearances

Legendary goalkeeper Steve 'Oggy' Ogrizovic was a popular stalwart of the Sky Blues side for 16 years after signing from Shrewsbury Town in 1984.

TOP

Three years later he was part of the team which won the FA Cup for the Sky Blues, making several vital saves during the final against Tottenham Hotspur at Wembley and in the semi-final against Leeds United.

Despite regular calls for international recognition, Oggy was never called up for England but that didn't matter to Coventry fans who saw the best of Ogrizovic in the regular battles against the drop the club had during the Premier League years.

Oggy famously scored for the Sky Blues from a goal kick against Sheffield Wednesday in 1986, and it was against the Owls that he made his final appearance in a 4-1 victory at Highfield Road in May 2000. Ogrizovic stayed with the Sky Blues and is currently the goalkeeping coach.

Conor Thomas was born on 29th October 1993...

1. Which international team has Thomas represented at U17 and U18 level?

2. When did Conor Thomas make his professional debut?

3. Conor attended Coundon Court School in Coventry, but which CCFC teammate went to school with him?

11 NOVEMBER

FRANCK MOUSSA CELEBRATES SCORING THE FOURTH GOAL IN A 5-0 WIN LAST NOVEMBER... BUT AGAINST WHO WERE WE PLAYING?

1.

2.

TWO OF OUR BOYS ARE DRESSED UP FOR CHRISTMAS... CAN YOU TELL WHO THEY ARE?

12 DECEMBER

The surnames of former Sky Blues' managers, dating back to the 1980s, are hidden in the grid, except for one...

can you work out who?

```
A T S B T R R K F M R D U E H
L O N Y D J S E X T O N Z S M
E Q I B K N O S S L I N A I C
P N B U T C H E R K G S E K A
C A O L N T X C B G M J Z A L
P D R M A T K I N S O N J F L
R P L D M C B L Y B R D E N I
E S A C E J K S O S E T T R S
S M M X L A W T E L I U J N T
S I B O O T H R O Y D G N E E
L R A K C J O A C F V L F I R
E T G P B H I C F B O R U W V
Y A K C A M W H B H H U P O D
H C W S I P L A E G O S A D G
F Q I T H O R N V S I T R U C
```

Steven **Pressley**	Iain **Dowie**	Roland **Nilsson**	Terry **Butcher**
Mark **Robins**	Micky **Adams**	Gordon **Strachan**	John **Sillett**
Andy **Thorn**	Peter **Reid**	Ron **Atkinson**	George **Curtis**
Aidy **Boothroyd**	Eric **Black**	Phil **Neal**	Don **Mackay**
Chris **Coleman**	Gary **McAllister**	Bobby **Gould**	Dave **Sexton**

44

Moldovan's Goal

ASTON VILLA 0-1 COVENTRY CITY

The Sky Blues finally beat their 62 year old Villa Park jinx on 14th February 1998 as a goal from Romanian striker Viorel Moldovan secured victory in the FA Cup fifth round.

Moldovan rarely figured regularly for the Sky Blues but the team were hit by injury and suspension and he was introduced as a sub ten minutes into the second half; seventeen minutes later he sealed his place in Coventry City history.

George Boateng picked up the ball in midfield, weaved past Wright, Southgate and Ehiogu in a mazy run before hitting a shot from distance. Villa Keeper Bosnich could only parry the ball into the path of Moldovan, who tapped in from four yards out.

MAGIC MOMENTS

Beating Man United

COVENTRY CITY 3-2 MANCHESTER UNITED

The Sky Blues shocked league champions and runaway leaders Manchester United in a thrilling 3-2 win at a packed and passionate Highfield Road on 28th December 1997.

City took the lead through Noel Whelan's side-footed finish early in the first half, but United levelled through Ole Gunnar Solskjaer before England striker Teddy Sheringham put the Red Devils into the lead after 47 minutes. With 86 minutes gone, it looked like the points were heading north before referee Neale Barry awarded the Sky Blues a penalty. Captain Dion Dublin stepped up to convert the spot kick and set the stage for a thrilling finale.

Two minutes later, pacy forward Darren Huckerby picked up the ball inside the United half, skipped past four United defenders and calmly slotted the ball past the onrushing keeper in front of the West Terrace to seal a legendary goal for himself and a legendary win for Gordon Strachan's side.

OLDHAM ATHLETIC

Ground: Boundary Park **Capacity:** 10,638
Manager: Lee Johnson **Nickname:** The Latics
Did you know: Boundary Park is less than 9 miles from the nearby stadiums of Bury, Manchester City, Manchester United and Rochdale.

PETERBOROUGH UNITED

Ground: London Road Stadium
Capacity: 14,640 **Manager:** Darren Ferguson
Nickname: The Posh **Did you know:** Peterborough United were relegated from the Championship on the final day of last season.

PORT VALE

Ground: Vale Park **Capacity:** 19,052 **Manager:** Micky Adams **Nicknames:** The Valiants, The Vale **Did you know:** Port Vale is one of the few English clubs not to be named after a city or town. It is a reference to a valley of ports on the Trent and Mersey Canal.

PRESTON NORTH END

Ground: Deepdale **Capacity:** 23,408 **Manager:** Simon Grayson **Nicknames:** The Lilywhites **Did you know:** Founding members of the Football League, they finished the first season as league champions. They also won the FA Cup that season and were first to achieve the English 'Double'.

ROTHERHAM UNITED

Ground: New York Stadium **Capacity:** 12,021
Manager: Steve Evans **Nicknames:** The Millers
Did you know: 'The Chuckle Brothers' were appointed as honorary presidents of Rotherham in 2007 in recognition of their contributions to the club.

SHEFFIELD UNITED

Ground: Bramall Lane **Capacity:** 32,702
Manager: David Weir **Nicknames:** The Blades, Red and White Army **Did you know:** The Club play their home games at Bramall Lane, the oldest major stadium in the world still hosting football matches.

SHREWSBURY TOWN

Ground: New Meadow **Capacity:** 9,875 **Manager:** Graham Turner **Nicknames:** Salop **Did you know:** Traditionally Walsall and Wolves were the club's major rivals. More recently, rivalry has grown with near-neighbours Hereford United and Chester City.

STEVENAGE

Ground: The Lamex Stadium **Capacity:** 6,722 **Manager:** Graham Westley **Nicknames:** The Boro **Did you know:** They were the first team to win a competitive final at the new Wembley Stadium in 2007, beating Kidderminster Harriers 3-2 to lift the FA Trophy.

SWINDON TOWN

Ground: County Ground **Capacity:** 14,700 **Manager:** Mark Cooper **Nicknames:** The Robins, The Reds, The Town **Did you know:** Swindon won promotion to the Premier League during the 1992-93 season, the only time the club has played in the top tier.

TRANMERE ROVERS

Ground: Prenton Park **Capacity:** 16,567 **Manager:** Ronnie Moore **Nicknames:** Superwhites, Rovers **Did you know:** Since the 1970s, Rovers have taken to the pitch to the theme music of US detective series 'The Rockford Files'.

WALSALL

Ground: Bescot Stadium **Capacity:** 11,300 **Manager:** Dean Smith **Nicknames:** The Saddlers **Did you know:** Their nickname, The Saddlers, reflects Walsall's status as a traditional centre for saddle manufacture.

WOLVERHAMPTON WANDERERS

Ground: Molineux **Capacity:** 30,852 **Manager:** Kenny Jackett **Nicknames:** Wolves **Did you know:** Wolves have won the FA Cup four times - in 1893, 1908, 1949 and 1960!

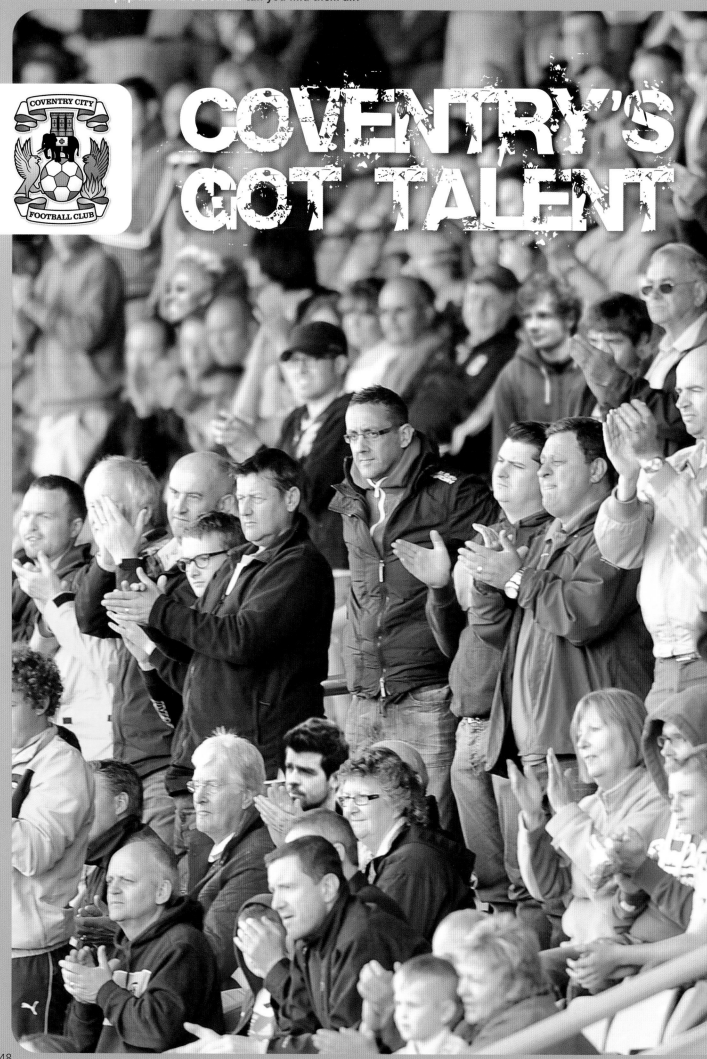

COVENTRY'S GOT TALENT

Set up a square within shooting distance of your goal. Place a keeper in goal, and a defender inside the square. You and the rest of your mates are attackers and should start at the other side of the square from the goal.

The purpose of this drill is to focus on dribbling to beat a defender and finishing with a shot on goal.

Remember to take turns being in goal so that everyone gets a chance to play all positions!

EASY

Dribble into the square and try to beat the defender and dribble out of the opposite side of the square.

If you successfully dribble through the square without losing the ball to the defender, finish with a shot on goal!

If you lose the ball to the defender or dribble out either side of the square, you must then switch places with the defender so that you are protecting the square and they become an attacker.

The next player in line can go as soon as a shot on goal is taken or the defender has won the ball.

HARD

Make the square bigger to make it harder for defenders or make the square smaller to make it harder for the attackers.

HARDER

You can make the square slightly larger and add a second defender so that the game becomes 2 v 1 and harder for the attacker.

To make shooting harder, move the square further away from the goal and encourage a longer shot.

DRILLS: ATTACKING

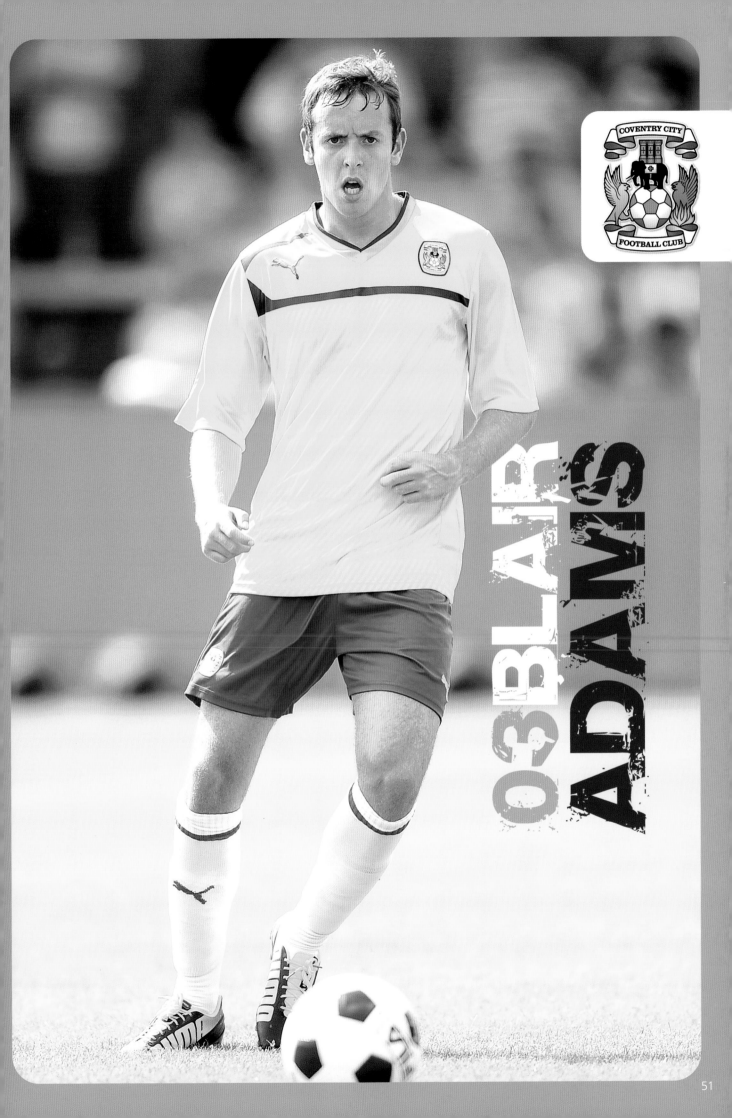

03 BLAIR ADAMS

51

CYRUS CHRISTIE

FAVOURITES

Favourite actor? Denzel Washington

Favourite actress? Salma Hayek

Favourite movie? Think Like A Man

Favourite musician or band? Jay Z

Favourite place? LA

YOUR TEAM MATES

Who is the best trainer? **Franck Moussa**

Who has the worst dress sense?

Lee Burge and Joe Murphy tied!

Who is the best dancer? **Mathieu Manset**

Who is the joker in the dressing room?

Callum Wilson

Who spends longest in front of the mirror?

Jordan Clarke

If you could trade places with someone for a day, who would it be?
Kevin Hart

If you were a character in any movie, who would it be?
King Leonidas (300) or Denzel in Man on Fire

Snow or (Sun?)
Coffee or (tea?)
Early bird or (night owl?)
Action or (comedy?)
(Apple) or Blackberry?
(Cowboys) or aliens?
(Skiing) or Snowboarding?
Sausage or bacon? *neither*
Cats or (dogs?)
(Bond) or Bourne?

What are your pet hates?
People standing on my trainers, mess, lack of hygiene

What do you do on your days off?
Chill or go out with teammates

If not a footballer, what would you be?
Basketball Player

BACK CHAT

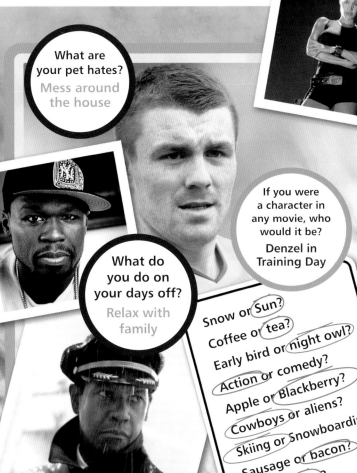

What are your pet hates? Mess around the house

What do you do on your days off? Relax with family

If you were a character in any movie, who would it be? Denzel in Training Day

JOHN FLECK

FAVOURITES

Favourite actor? Denzel Washington

Favourite actress? Angelina Jolie

Favourite movie? Flight

Favourite musician or band? 50 Cent

Favourite place? Glasgow

YOUR TEAM MATES

Who is the best trainer?
Franck Moussa or Carl Baker

Who has the worst dress sense?
Lee Burge or Joe Murphy

Who is the best dancer? **Jordan Willis**

Who is the joker in the dressing room? **Joe Murphy**

Who spends longest in front of the mirror? **Leon Clarke**

Snow or (Sun?)
Coffee or (tea?)
Early bird or (night owl?)
(Action) or comedy?
Apple or (Blackberry?)
(Cowboys) or aliens?
(Skiing) or Snowboarding?
Sausage or (bacon?)
Cats or (dogs?)
(Bond) or Bourne?

BLAIR ADAMS

FAVOURITES

Favourite actor? Denzel Washington

Favourite actress? Kate Beckinsale

Favourite movie? Goodfellas

Favourite musician or band? Kings Of Leon

Favourite place? South Shields

YOUR TEAM MATES

Who is the best trainer?
Carl Baker

Who has the worst dress sense?
Joe Murphy

Who is the best dancer?
Franck Moussa

Who is the joker in the dressing room? **Carl Baker**

Who spends longest in front of the mirror? **John Fleck**

What are your pet hates? Leaving the milk out of the fridge

If you could trade places with someone for a day, who would it be? David Beckham

Snow or (Sun?)
(Coffee) or tea?
(Early bird) or night owl?
Action or (comedy?)
(Apple) or Blackberry?
Cowboys or (aliens?)
(Skiing) or Snowboarding?
(Sausage) or bacon?
Cats or (dogs?)
(Bond) or Bourne?

If you were a character in any movie, who would it be? Neo in the Matrix

53

FACT OR FIB?

7

Sky Blue Sam was originally a rhinoceros.

1. FACT OR FIB?

Coventry City were formed in 1883 as Singers FC.

2. FACT OR FIB?

The Sky Blues top goalscorer of all time is Clarrie Bourton with a total of 179 goals!

3. FACT OR FIB?

Franck Moussa was born in Debrecen, Hungary.

4. FACT OR FIB?

Before coming to Coventry, Steven Pressley was manger at Falkirk.

5. FACT OR FIB?

In the last game of 2013, Sky Blues face Oldham.

6. FACT OR FIB?

John Fleck is a great defender, he made 42 appearances for the club last season.

7. FACT OR FIB?

Young midfielder, Adam Barton has been capped at U21 level by Republic of Ireland.

8. FACT OR FIB?

Highfield Road was home to the Sky Blues for 97 years.

9. FACT OR FIB?

Coventry City signed former Reading striker Mathieu Manset on a one-year deal, with an option for a further year in August 2013.

10. FACT OR FIB?

Coventry consider their biggest rival to be Leicester, with whom they play the M69 Derby.

11. FACT OR FIB?

Coventry City's highest goalscorer last season was Carl Baker.

12. FACT OR FIB?

Coventry won the FA Cup in 1987 against Liverpool.

13. FACT OR FIB?

Striker Billy Daniels, celebrated his 19th birthday this July.

14. FACT OR FIB?

Coventry's top appearance maker of all time is George Curtis.

15. FACT OR FIB?

Andy Webster is from Dundee, Ireland.

16. FACT OR FIB?

Jimmy Hill was a Sky Blues manager of the 1980s.

17. FACT OR FIB?

The last goal at Highfield Road was scored by Andrew Whing.

18. FACT OR FIB?

Coventry's youngest ever player was Jonson Clarke-Harris, 16 years 20 days, as a substitute vs Morecambe, 2010.

19. FACT OR FIB?

'Keeper, Joe Murphy, is a Republic of Ireland international.

20. FACT OR FIB?

DERBY DAYS

VILLA 1 SKY BLUES 4

PREMIERSHIP, FEBRUARY 27TH 1999

This was a simply stunning victory watched by just under 40,000 at Villa Park as Gordon Strachan's side ran riot. John Aloisi and George Boateng both went into the match with just a solitary goal to each of their names for the season but both tripled their tally with a pair of superbly taken braces.

Aussie Aloisi opened the scoring mid-way through the first half with a clever left foot shot across Villa 'keeper Michael Oakes. Boateng doubled the lead six minutes into the second half scoring from a tight angle after a low right wing cross from speed merchant Darren Huckerby.

Villa were quickly back in the game though through a penalty smashed beyond Magnus Hedman by former Sky Blue Dion Dublin after Richard Shaw fouled Julian Joachim. City drew on all their experience to weather the Villa storm as the home side looked for an equaliser before Aloisi restored the two goal cushion in the 73rd minute with a spectacular volley from Steve Froggatt's left wing free kick.

Extending the lead further, Boateng made it 4-1 nine minutes from time in front of the delirious City fans. Sent clear by Gary McAllister's through ball, Boateng outpaced the home defence making contact just outside the box as Oakes rushed out.

LEICESTER CITY 1-3 SKY BLUES

PREMIERSHIP, APRIL 7TH 2001

Separated by 24 miles along the M69, Sky Blues rivalry with Leicester has grown in recent years. Few games between the clubs have been more important than this one, with the league table looking none too clever as the season headed towards its climax. Coventry manager Gordon Strachan had made it clear that three points were essential.

Craig Bellamy put the visitors ahead in the very first minute after great work from Mustapha Hadji. Distinctly second best, Leicester drew level against the run of play with an eighth minute equaliser from Ade Akinbiyi but the Sky Blues weren't to be denied. Lee Carsley restored the lead 10 minutes later with a well-taken header from Barry Quinn's cross from the right flank.

Over-run in the first half, Leicester were expected to mount a strong challenge after the break but Coventry simply maintained their superiority. Six minutes after the re-start they extended their lead, appropriately courtesy of John Hartson whose determination to win his personal contest with home captain Matt Elliott typified Coventry's spirit. Hartson headed home a corner from Paul Telfer.

High flying Leicester were well beaten as the Sky Blues wracked up back to back league wins for the first time since the opening week of the season. It was the best away win of the season and completed a seasonal double over Leicester in what was a poor season overall for the Sky Blues.

SKY BLUES 1-0 LEICESTER CITY

PREMIERSHIP, DECEMBER 10TH 2000

Just one goal was sufficient to secure three important points as Sky Blues brought a bad run of one point from seven games to a well timed end with victory against Leicester on a day when Republic of Ireland international midfielder Lee Carsley made his debut after his transfer from Blackburn Rovers.

Derbies are passionate affairs and Craig Bellamy and Robbie Savage clashed fiercely early on but Bellamy had the final word when his 40th minute header won the game. The Wales international's movement out-foxed Leicester defender Frank Sinclair as Bellamy capitalized on Paul Telfer's cross.

Moroccan Mustapha Hadji went closest to doubling the lead with a 74th minute shot after great work from Gary Breen but one goal and a well-deserved clean sheet ensured the spoils.

SKY BLUES 3-0 VILLA

PREMIER LEAGUE, DECEMBER 26TH 1992

Mick Quinn's ninth and tenth goals for the club in just his sixth game inflicted the heaviest defeat of the season so far for Villa, with Quinn turning provider to create the final goal for Robert Rosario. All of the goals came in a scintillating seven-minute spell just before the hour mark as City made it the merriest of Christmases for all Sky Blues supporters.

Two of the goals stemmed from throw ins. Kenny Sansom's throw was worked into the box where from Rosario's header Quinn hooked a volley beyond visiting 'keeper Nigel Spink. Three minutes later Kevin Gallacher and Rosario combined to provide goal machine Quinn with a chance to net with a first time right foot shot. Four minutes further into the game and Villa were finished off when from another throw in Peter Atherton found Quinn who turned provider for Rosario whose first time left foot finish put his name onto the score-line to go with his two assists.

A minute from time Quinn was subbed to a hero's welcome from the Highfield Road faithful.

SKY BLUES 2 LEICESTER CITY 0

CHAMPIONSHIP, FEBRUARY 23RD 2008

Leicester manager Ian Holloway complained about what he described as "One of the maddest decisions I have ever seen" but whether he liked it or not the award of a 32nd minute penalty after Gareth McAuley fouled Leon Best enabled Elliott Ward to step up, keep his cool and convert the spot kick for his first league goal in just under a year.

There was no arguing about Best's second major contribution to the game when the striker finished off a clever pass from Kevin Thornton to wrap up the victory 11 minutes from time in a match that got new Coventry manager Chris Coleman off to a winning start.

DERBY HERO · PAUL TELFER

Paul Telfer played more games for Coventry than any other club in his career. Always a hard-working team player whether in midfield or at full back, Paul didn't often hog the headlines but was nonetheless an important part of any success City achieved in his half dozen years at the club from 1995 to 2001.

Paul scored in a 3-0 FA Cup away win at Leicester in 1999 and in the 2000-01 season when the double was done over The Foxes, he created goals in both fixtures, his cross teeing up Craig Bellamy for the only goal of the game at home while his corner set up John Hartson for the third goal in the away victory. In December 1997 he'd played his part in a solid 2-0 win at Leicester while he was also part of the victorious Sky Blues side who trounced Aston Villa 4-1 at Villa Park in 1999.

Telfer was capped once by Scotland and it was during his spell at Coventry, he appeared against France at Hampden Park in March 2000. Paul's contribution at Coventry wasn't forgotten by Gordon Strachan or Gary McAllister. Strachan later signed him for Southampton; where he played in the 2003 FA Cup final, and Celtic, where he won two league titles and the Scottish League Cup. After Paul's return to England, McAllister later took him to Leeds United.

09 LEON
CLARKE

Each creature represents a football club... **can you name every one?**

FOOTIE

ABOUT

WILD

ANSWERS ON PAGE 62

59

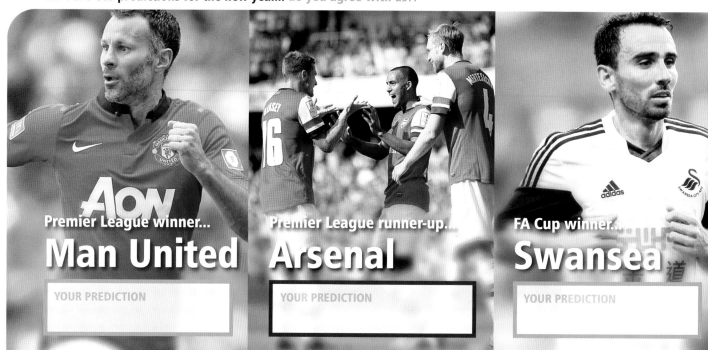

Premier League winner...
Man United
YOUR PREDICTION

Premier League runner-up...
Arsenal
YOUR PREDICTION

FA Cup winner...
Swansea
YOUR PREDICTION

2014 PREDICTIONS

League 1 winner...
Coventry City
YOUR PREDICTION

League 1 runner-up...
MK Dons
YOUR PREDICTION

Championship winner...
Boro
YOUR PREDICTION

Championship runner-up...
Derby County
YOUR PREDICTION

League Cup winner...
Everton
YOUR PREDICTION

World Cup 2014 winners...
Brazil

YOUR PREDICTION

2014 Manager of the Year...
Steven Pressley

YOUR PREDICTION

First player to get sent off in 2014...
Joey Barton

YOUR PREDICTION

First player booked for taking their top off in 2014...
Luis Suarez

YOUR PREDICTION

First Coventry player to score three goals in 2014...
Billy Daniels

YOUR PREDICTION

First player to score a hat-trick in 2014...
Robin van Persie

YOUR PREDICTION

League 1 top scorer...
Leon Clarke

YOUR PREDICTION

Premier League top scorer...
Christian Benteke

YOUR PREDICTION

ANSWERS

PAGE 20
BIG FAT QUIZ OF THE YEAR

JANUARY: Chris Robertson (o.g.)
FEBRUARY: 1. 10, 2.False, 6'2",
3. Wolverhampton Wanderers
MARCH: 1. Falkirk, 2. False, Scotland,
3. 271 **APRIL:** Franck Moussa
MAY: 1. Coventry 3, Tottenham 2,
2. John Sillett, 3. Bennett, Houchen
and Mabbutt (o.g.), 4. 96,000,
5. Steve Ogrizovic **JUNE:** 1. Arnhem,
Holland, 2. Ryton training ground

PAGE 36
GUESS WHO?

1. Blair Adams, 2. Cyrus Christie,
3. Jordan Willis, 4.John Fleck,
5.Mathieu Manset, 6. Carl Baker,
7. Louis Garner, 8.Adam Barton

PAGE 39
FACE OFF

1. Billy Daniels, 2. Carl Baker,
3. Jordan Willis, 4. Leon Clarke,
5. Adam Barton, 6. John Fleck,
7. Lee Burge, 8. Cyrus Christie,
9. Callum Wilson

PAGE 42
BIG FAT QUIZ OF THE YEAR

JULY: Callum Wilson **AUGUST:** 1. 1883,
2. Jonson Clarke-Harris, 3. Shrewsbury
SEPTEMBER: 1. Nuneaton Town and Hinckley
United, 2. 10 August 2010 v Morecambe,
3. True **OCTOBER:** 1. England, 2. 8 January
2011 in a 2-1 FA Cup win over Crystal Palace,
3. Jordan Clarke **NOVEMBER:** Hartlepool
United **DECEMBER:** 1. Blair Adams,
2. Leon Clarke

PAGE 44
CAN YOU MANAGE?

John Sillett

PAGE 48
COVENTRY'S GOT TALENT

Ollie Murs, Ed Sheeran, Robin Thicke,
Rita Ora and Emeli Sande

PAGE 54
FACT OR FIB?

1. Fib, 2. Fact, 3. Fib, 182 goals, 4. Fib,
Brussels, Belgium, 5. Fact, 6. Fact,
7. Fib, Fleck is a midfielder, 8. Fact,
9. Fib, 106 years, 10. Fact, 11. Fact,
12. Fact, 13. Fib, against Tottenham
Hotspur, 14. Fact, 15. Fib, Steve
Ogrizovic, 16. Fib, Dundee Scotland,
17.Fib, 1960s, 18.Fact, 19. Fact,
20. Fact

PAGE 59
WILD ABOUT FOOTIE

1. Leicester City, 2. Newcastle
United, 3. Norwich, 4. Millwall,
5. Sheffield Wednesday, 6. Watford,
7. Wolverhampton Wanderers,
8. Derby County, 9. Hull,
10. Sunderland